Saint Michael

Novena and Prayers

By
Mary Mark Wickenhiser, FSP

Pauline
BOOKS & MEDIA
Boston

Nihil Obstat: Rev. Thomas W. Buckley, STD, SSL

Imprimatur: ✠ Most Rev. Seán O'Malley, O.F.M.Cap.
Archbishop of Boston
June 14, 2004

ISBN 0-8198-7088-9

Cover art: Tom Kinarney

Texts of the New Testament used in this work are taken from *The New Testament: St. Paul Catholic Edition,* translated by Mark A. Wauck, copyright © 2000, Society of St. Paul, Staten Island, New York, and used by permission. All rights reserved.

Texts of the Psalms used in this work are translated by Manuel Miguens. Copyright © 1995, Daughters of St. Paul.

All rights reserved. No part of this book may be reproduced or transmitted in any form or by any means, electronic or mechanical, including photocopying, recording or by any information storage and retrieval system, without permission in writing from the publisher.

"P" and PAULINE are registered trademarks of the Daughters of St. Paul

Copyright © 2004, Daughters of St. Paul

Published by Pauline Books & Media, 50 Saint Pauls Avenue, Boston MA 02130-3491.

Printed in Canada

www.pauline.org

Pauline Books & Media is the publishing house of the Daughters of St. Paul, an international congregation of women religious serving the Church with the communications media.

1 2 3 4 5 6 7 8   11 10 09 08 07 06 05 04

Contents

What Is a Novena? --------------------- 4

St. Michael --------------------------- 7

Morning Prayer ---------------------- 11

Novena to St. Michael ------------- 16

Prayers for Various Needs -------- 25

Evening Prayer ---------------------- 34

What Is a Novena?

The Catholic tradition of praying novenas has its roots in the earliest days of the Church. In the Acts of the Apostles we read that after the ascension of Jesus, the apostles returned to Jerusalem, to the upper room, where "They all devoted themselves single-mindedly to prayer, along with some women and Mary the Mother of Jesus and his brothers" (Acts 1:14). Jesus had instructed his disciples to wait for the coming of the Holy Spirit, and on the day of Pentecost, the Spirit of the Lord came to them. This prayer of the first Christian community was the first "novena." Based on this, Christians have always prayed for various needs, trusting that God both hears and answers prayer.

The word "novena" is derived from the Latin term *novem*, meaning nine. In biblical times numbers held deep symbolism for people. The number "three," for example, symbolized perfection, fullness, completeness. The number nine—three times three—symbolized perfection times perfection. Novenas developed because it was thought that—symbolically speaking—nine days represented the perfect amount of time to pray. The ancient Greeks and Romans had the custom of mourning for nine days after a death. The early Christian Church offered Mass for the deceased for nine consecutive days. During the Middle Ages novenas in preparation for solemn feasts became popular, as did novenas to particular saints.

Whether a novena is made solemnly—in a parish church in preparation for a feastday—or in the privacy of one's home, as Christians we never really pray alone. Through the waters of Baptism we have become members of the Body of Christ and are thereby united to every other member of Christ's Mystical Body. When we pray, we are spiritually united with all the other members.

Just as we pray for each other while here on earth, those who have gone before us and are united with God in heaven can pray for us and intercede for us as well. We Catholics use the term "communion of saints" to refer to this exchange of spiritual help among the members of the Church on earth, those who have died and are being purified, and the saints in heaven.

While nothing can replace the celebration of Mass and the sacraments as the Church's highest form of prayer, devotions have a special place in

Catholic life. Devotions such as the Stations of the Cross can help us enter into the sufferings of Jesus and give us an understanding of his personal love for us. The mysteries of the rosary can draw us into meditating on the lives of Jesus and Mary. Devotions to the saints can help us witness to our faith and encourage us in our commitment to lead lives of holiness and service as they did.

How to use this booklet

The morning and evening prayers are modeled on the Liturgy of the Hours, following its pattern of psalms, Scripture readings, and intercessions.

We suggest that during the novena you make time in your schedule to pray the morning prayer and evening prayer. If you are able, try to also set aside a time during the day when you can pray the novena and any other particular prayer(s) you have chosen. Or you can recite the devotional prayers at the conclusion of the morning or evening prayer. What is important is to pray with expectant faith and confidence in a loving God who will answer our prayers in the way that will most benefit us. The Lord "satisfies the thirsty, and the hungry he fills with good things" (Ps 107:9).

St. Michael

Guardian of God's People, Protector Against Evil, Patron of Police Officers

The Church honors St. Michael as one of the most important angels in heaven. Angels are purely spiritual beings, and as such they do not have bodies. These spiritual creatures have intelligence and free will; they are personal and immortal, and surpass in perfection all visible creatures (cf. nn. 328, 330, *Catechism of the Catholic Church*). The angels are servants and messengers of God. From Scripture we learn that angels heralded the birth of Christ, announcing this good news to shepherds watching their flocks (Lk 2:8–16). Angels ministered to Jesus during his agony in the garden (Lk 22:43), and they announced that Jesus had risen (Mt 28:3–8). When Peter was in prison for having preached about Jesus, an angel led him out to freedom (Acts 12:6–10).

The Opening Prayer of the Mass for the feast of Saints Michael, Gabriel, and Raphael, archangels (September 29), draws our attention to the angels in relation to us. We ask God to grant that these spiritual beings, who serve him in heaven, may watch over us, keep us safe from danger, and help us through the difficult moments of our lives.

In the Prayer over the Gifts we are reminded that the angels help us to praise God. Although we can't see them, they bring our prayers of sacrifice and praise to the throne of the Most High. And, at every Mass, the Church on earth joins its praise to that of the angels, as we pray the "Holy, holy, holy...."

St. Michael in Scripture

Apocalyptic literature in the Bible awards the archangel Michael a prominent role in passages that refer to the end-time. In the Old Testament Book of Daniel we read: "At that time Michael, the great prince, the protector of your people, shall arise" (Dn 12:1; see also 10:13). The New Testament Book of Revelation continues the theme of Michael as the protector of God's people and consequently the adversary of Satan: "Then war broke out in Heaven. Michael and his angels fought against the dragon. The dragon and his angels fought back but they were defeated and no longer had a place in Heaven. Then the huge dragon—the ancient serpent who is called the Devil and Satan, who deceived the whole world—was thrown down to earth and his angels were thrown down with him" (12:7–9). The Letter of Jude refers to Michael disputing with the devil over the body of Moses (Jude, vs. 9). While apocalyptic writing can be difficult to interpret, and need not be taken literally, it indicates that Michael holds a primary place in the battle against evil. These Scripture passages form the basis for devotion to the archangel Michael. In referring to the fall of the angels, the *Catechism of the Catholic Church* states: "We find a reflection of that rebellion in the tempter's words to our first parents: 'You will be like God'" (n. 392). Michael, instead, chose to worship and adore God alone. The very name *Mi-cha-el* means "Who is like God?"

Devotion to St. Michael, invoked as the Protector of the Church against the power of Satan, has grown steadily throughout the centuries. In France, the sanctuary of Mont-St. Michel in Normandy, begun in the eighth century, was a popular place of pilgrimage for centuries. (Today it is preserved as a historical monument.) History tells of various saints who have had a great devotion to St. Michael. For example, St. Lawrence Justinian wrote: "Let all acknowledge St. Michael as their protector, and be devoted to him.... He guards us through life, directs us on our way, and conducts us to our eternal home." St. Joan of Arc, who had a vision of the archangel, ascribed her vocation and her victories to St. Michael, the patron of France.

In the 1880s, during a difficult period in the Church, Pope Leo XIII decreed that the prayer to St. Michael be recited by all the faithful at the end of Mass. Although with the renewal of the liturgy this practice has been discontinued, we can still pray privately for St. Michael's help in overcoming the forces of evil in our world.

Marianne Lorraine Trouvé, FSP

Morning Prayer

Morning prayer is a time to give praise and thanks to God, to remind ourselves that he is the source of all beauty and goodness. Lifting one's heart and mind to God in the early hours of the day puts one's life into perspective: God is our loving Creator who watches over us with tenderness and is always ready to embrace us with his compassion and mercy.

While at prayer, try to create a prayerful atmosphere, perhaps with a burning candle to remind you that Christ is the light who illumines your daily path, an open Bible to remind you that the Lord is always present, a crucifix to remind you of the depths of God's love for you. Soft music can also contribute to a serene and prayerful mood.

If a quiet place is not available, or if you pray as you commute to and from work, remember that the God who loves you is present everywhere and hears your prayer no matter the setting.

I will bless the Lord at all times.
His praise will be ever on my lips.
Glory to the Father, and to the Son, and to the
 Holy Spirit,
as it was in the beginning, is now, and will be
 forever. Amen.

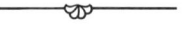

Psalm 34

Look to God and be radiant with joy.

I will bless the Lord at all times;
his praise is ever on my lips.
It is in the Lord that my soul shall boast.
The humble shall hear of it and rejoice.
Join me in celebrating the greatness of the Lord,
and let us extol his name together.

I sought the Lord and he answered me;
he delivered me from all my fears.
Those who gazed on him were radiant with joy
and their faces were not made to blush.
The afflicted ones cried out and the Lord heard,
and saved them from all their troubles.
The angel of the Lord is encamped
'round those who fear and delivers them.
Taste and see how good the Lord is.

Happy the one who takes refuge in him.

Glory to the Father....

The Word of God
Ephesians 6:10–11, 13–18

Although the ultimate victory over evil has been won through the "blood of the Lamb," Jesus, we still need to continue in our struggle against the forces of sin and evil that impact our lives. As God's messenger, St. Michael stands by us, offering the assurance of God's love and abiding help, and strengthening us with the spiritual means to remain steadfast in virtue.

Become strong through the Lord's power and might. Put on God's armor so you will be able to stand up against the schemes of the Devil.... Gird your loins with truth and put on the breastplate of righteousness. Put on your feet the boots of preparedness for the good news of peace. And along with all this take up the shield of the faith, with which you will be able to extinguish all the flaming arrows of the Evil One. Take the helmet of salvation and the sword of the Spirit, which is the word of God.

I hope in the Lord. I trust in God's word.

From prayer one draws the strength needed to meet the challenges of daily life as a committed follower of Jesus Christ, and, as such, to be a living sign of the Lord's loving presence in the world.

Intercessions

God, Father and Creator, I thank you for your mercies, which grace us at the beginning of this day. I trust in your loving care, and with confidence I place my petitions before you:

Response: *Lord, lead me along the right path.*

Help me to be aware of your abiding presence, that I may walk with you throughout this day and see you in all whom I meet. **R.**

Give me a generous heart that I may respond with compassion to those who may seek my help today. **R.**

Grant me the strength to do good and the courage to walk away from temptation. **R.**

Sustain me with a spirit of hope when faced with hardship and tribulation. **R.**

Watch over my loved ones, family, and friends this day. **R.**

(Add your own general intentions and your particular intentions for this novena.)

Conclude your intercessions by praying to our Heavenly Father in the words Jesus taught us:

Our Father, who art in heaven, hallowed be thy name; thy kingdom come; thy will be done on earth as it is in heaven. Give us this day our daily bread, and forgive us our trespasses, as we forgive those who trespass against us, and lead us not into temptation, but deliver us from evil. Amen.

Closing Prayer

Gracious Lord, as I begin this day let your constant love and ever-watchful care be with me. Bless my words and actions and accept them as an offering of my love and gratitude. I ask this through Jesus Christ, your Son. Amen.

Let us praise the Lord.

And give him thanks.

Novena to St. Michael*

First Day

St. Michael, reflection of God's beauty, holiness, and majesty,

—intercede for us before God's holy throne.

You are the chosen protector of all God's people,

— present my prayer of praise and supplication at the throne of God.

O God, through the intercession of St. Michael and the heavenly choir of the Seraphim, instill in my heart the flame of charity, that I may

---

* On each day of the novena we invoke St. Michael and a particular "choir" of angels, such as the Seraphim, Cherubim, etc., to seek their protection and help along life's journey. The nine "choirs" of angels, grouped according to their activity or function in Scripture, were first mentioned in Church writings as early as the fifth century.

love you with my whole heart and seek to love others as you love me. Keep me faithful to your love today and open my heart to receive the blessings you want to pour out on me, especially the grace that I ask for at this time.

(Mention your petition and pray one Our Father, Hail Mary, and Glory to the Father...)

Our Father, who art in heaven, hallowed be thy name; thy kingdom come; thy will be done on earth as it is in heaven. Give us this day our daily bread, and forgive us our trespasses, as we forgive those who trespass against us, and lead us not into temptation, but deliver us from evil. Amen.

Hail Mary, full of grace, the Lord is with you. Blessed are you among women, and blessed is the fruit of your womb, Jesus. Holy Mary, Mother of God, pray for us sinners, now and at the hour of our death. Amen.

Glory to the Father, and to the Son, and to the Holy Spirit, as it was in the beginning, is now, and will be forever. Amen.

Second Day

St. Michael, reflection of God's beauty, holiness, and majesty,

—intercede for us before God's holy throne.

You are the chosen protector of all God's people,

— present my prayer of praise and supplication at the throne of God.

O God, through the intercession of St. Michael and the heavenly choir of the Cherubim, grant that I may leave aside all that may lead me to sin and follow only the path of Christian holiness. Keep me faithful to your love today and open my heart to receive the blessings you want to pour out on me, especially the grace that I ask for at this time.

(Mention your petition and pray one Our Father, Hail Mary, and Glory to the Father… See page 17ff.)

Third Day

St. Michael, reflection of God's beauty, holiness, and majesty,

—intercede for us before God's holy throne.

You are the chosen protector of all God's people,

— present my prayer of praise and supplication at the throne of God.

O God, through the intercession of St. Michael and the heavenly choir of the Thrones, fill my heart with a sincere spirit of gentleness and humility. Keep me faithful to your love today and open my heart to receive the blessings you want to pour out on me, especially the grace that I ask for at this time.

(Mention your petition and pray one Our Father, Hail Mary, and Glory to the Father… See page 17ff.)

Fourth Day

St. Michael, reflection of God's beauty, holiness, and majesty,

—intercede for us before God's holy throne.

You are the chosen protector of all God's people,

— present my prayer of praise and supplication at the throne of God.

O God, through the intercession of St. Michael and the heavenly choir of the Dominions, grant that I may ever keep control over my senses so that my thoughts, words, and actions may always serve your kingdom here on earth. Keep me faithful to your love today and open my heart to receive the blessings you want to pour out on me, especially the grace that I ask for at this time.

(Mention your petition and pray one Our Father, Hail Mary, and Glory to the Father... See page 17ff.)

Fifth Day

St. Michael, *reflection of God's beauty, holiness, and majesty,*

—intercede for us before God's holy throne.

You are the chosen protector of all God's people,

— present my prayer of praise and supplication at the throne of God.

O God, through the intercession of St. Michael and the heavenly choir of the Powers, keep temptation far from me and defend me against the deceits of the Evil One. Keep me faithful to your love today and open my heart to receive the blessings you want to pour out on me, especially the grace that I ask for at this time.

(Mention your petition and pray one Our Father, Hail Mary, and Glory to the Father... See page 17ff.)

Sixth Day

St. Michael, *reflection of God's beauty, holiness, and majesty,*

—intercede for us before God's holy throne.

You are the chosen protector of all God's people,

— present my prayer of praise and supplication at the throne of God.

O God, through the intercession of St. Michael and the heavenly choir of the Virtues, lead me along the path to holiness of life that I may love and serve others in your name. Keep me faithful to your love today and open my heart to receive the blessings you want to pour out on me, especially the grace that I ask for at this time.

(Mention your petition and pray one Our Father, Hail Mary, and Glory to the Father... See page 17ff.)

Seventh Day

St. Michael, reflection of God's beauty, holiness, and majesty,

—intercede for us before God's holy throne.

You are the chosen protector of all God's people,

— present my prayer of praise and supplication at the throne of God.

O God, through the intercession of St. Michael and the heavenly choir of the Principalities, fill my heart with a spirit of true and sincere obedience and increase my desire to do your will in all things. Keep me faithful to your love today and open my heart to receive the blessings you want to pour out on me, especially the grace that I ask for at this time.

(Mention your petition and pray one Our Father, Hail Mary, and Glory to the Father… See page 17ff.)

Eighth Day

St. Michael, reflection of God's beauty, holiness, and majesty,

—intercede for us before God's holy throne.

You are the chosen protector of all God's people,

— present my prayer of praise and supplication at the throne of God.

O God, through the intercession of St. Michael and the heavenly choir of the Archangels, increase my faith and grant me perseverance in doing good works that I may enjoy everlasting life in your presence. Keep me faithful to your love today and open my heart to receive the blessings you want to pour out on me, especially the grace that I ask for at this time.

(Mention your petition and pray one Our Father, Hail Mary, and Glory to the Father... See page 17ff.)

Ninth Day

St. Michael, reflection of God's beauty, holiness, and majesty,

—intercede for us before God's holy throne.

You are the chosen protector of all God's people,

— present my prayer of praise and supplication at the throne of God.

O God, through the intercession of St. Michael and the heavenly choir of the Angels, keep me and my loved ones from sin and evil here on earth, and after death lead us into the everlasting joy of heaven. Keep me faithful to your love today and open my heart to receive the blessings you want to pour out on me, especially the grace that I ask for at this time.

(Mention your petition and pray one Our Father, Hail Mary, and Glory to the Father... See page 17ff.)

Prayers for Various Needs

To St. Michael, Protector of God's People

"Pope Leo XIII introduced a special prayer to St. Michael throughout the Church. Although this prayer is no longer recited at the end of Mass, I ask everyone not to forget it and to recite it to obtain help in the battle against forces of darkness and against the spirit of this world."

(Pope John Paul II, Sunday, April 24, 1994)

St. Michael, the Archangel, defend us in the battle. Be our defense against the wickedness and deceit of the devil. May God rebuke him, we humbly pray. And you, O Prince of the heavenly host, by the power of God banish into hell Satan and the other evil spirits who roam through the world seeking the ruin of souls. Amen.

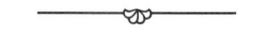

Prayer in Time of Difficulty

Glorious St. Michael, Prince of the heavenly hosts, valiant defender of the Church, you are always ready to assist the People of God in time of adversity. Be with me now in my hour of difficulty that I may walk steadfastly along the way of discipleship. I have confidence that through your intercession the Lord will grant me all the spiritual graces and strength that I need to follow Jesus more closely, and that one day I may rejoice forever with you in heaven. Amen.

Prayer for Perseverance

O God, you made blessed Michael, your Archangel, victorious in the battle against evil. We ask that, with the cross of your Son as our banner, we too may be victorious in the spiritual conflicts we face in our daily lives. Through the intercession of St. Michael, deliver us from all evil and keep temptation far from us. Guide us to faithfully follow your will and to walk in the way of your commandments. We ask this through Christ, our Lord. Amen.

Prayer for the Church

Glorious St. Michael, guardian and defender of the Church of Jesus Christ, come to the assistance of the Church in this time of need. Guard the Pope with special care, and intercede for him that he may carry out his ministry in peace and joy. Obtain for bishops the spiritual gifts necessary to be true shepherds of the flocks given to their care. Ask God to give our priests the courage they need to meet the challenges of their vocation. For men and women religious, ask that they be granted enthusiasm for their calling and a loving reverence for all those whom they serve in their varied ministries. For the laity in the Church, ask for the gift of fidelity to Christ and to their call to discipleship. For those who have distanced themselves from the Church, inspire them to undertake the interior journey that will lead them back to the grace of the sacraments. For all Christians, ask for the gift of unity, and ask the Holy Spirit to inspire the hearts of all people to continue the saving work of Christ until the end of time when we will all be united in heaven. Amen.

Prayer for Police Officers

St. Michael, defender against the forces of evil, protect our police officers and sustain them in their never-ending struggle to defeat criminal forces in our society. Ask the Lord to keep them safe and to give them courage in the face of danger, right judgment in the face of confusion, and clarity in the face of ambiguity. Inspire them to safeguard human dignity, and keep their hearts free from anger and bitterness when confronted with so much wrongdoing.

Encourage them to be compassionate with those who are hurting and give them self-control when confronting perpetrators. Be their constant companion and keep them safe from temptation and harm. Teach them how to live by faith in Jesus' promise that he is with us always. Teach them how to live in hope, relying on the Lord's saving power to bring them through hard times. Teach them how to live in Jesus' love that they may be light in the darkness for others.

Trusting in your powerful intercession before the throne of God, I ask that you guide all law enforcement officers along life's journey until the day they join you and all the angels in heaven to praise God for all eternity. Amen.

Police Officer's Prayer to St. Michael

St. Michael, defender against the forces of evil, protect all police officers and sustain us in our never-ending struggle to defeat criminal forces in our society. Ask the Lord to keep us safe and to give us courage in the face of danger, right judgment in the face of confusion, and clarity in the face of ambiguity. Inspire us to safeguard human dignity, and keep our hearts free from anger and bitterness when confronted with so much wrongdoing.

Encourage us to be compassionate with those who are hurting and give us self-control when confronting perpetrators. Be our constant companion and keep us safe from temptation and harm. Teach us how to live by faith in Jesus' promise that he is with us always. Teach us how to live in hope, relying on the Lord's saving power to bring us through hard times. Teach us how to live in Jesus' love that we may be light in the darkness for others.

Trusting in your powerful intercession before the throne of God, I take you as my protector and guide along life's journey, relying on the Lord's loving care that I may know his power working in my life until the day I join you and all the angels in heaven to praise God for all eternity. Amen.

Prayer for One's Family

Heavenly Father, I thank you for the gift of my family and for the many joys and blessings that have come to me through each of them. Help me to appreciate the uniqueness of each while celebrating the diversity of all. Through the intercession of St. Michael, I ask you to protect my family from the evils of this world. Grant us all the power to forgive when we have been hurt, and the humility to ask for forgiveness when we have caused pain. Unite us in the love of your Son, Jesus, that we may be a sign of the unity you desire for all humankind.

St. Michael, intercede for us. Amen.

Prayer for a Holy Death

St. Michael, light and confidence of souls at the hour of death, I ask you to intercede for all the dying, and invoke your assistance in the hour of my own death. Deliver me from sudden death; obtain for me the grace to live as a faithful disciple of Jesus, to detach my heart from everything worldly, and daily to gather treasures for the moment of my death. Obtain for me the grace to receive the sacraments of the sick well, and at the moment of my death fill my heart with sentiments of faith, hope, love, and sorrow for sins, so that I may breathe forth my soul in peace. Amen.

Adapted from the writings of Blessed James Alberione

Prayer of Praise and Thanksgiving

It is fitting for us to praise and thank God for the graces and privileges he has bestowed upon his angels and saints. Devotees of St. Michael may pray the following act of thanksgiving during their novena.

All-loving God, I praise, glorify, and bless you for all the graces and privileges you have bestowed upon your messenger and servant, St. Michael. By the merits of your angels grant me your grace, and through the intercession of your Archangel Michael help me in all my needs. At the hour of my death be with me until that time when I can join the angels and saints in heaven to praise you forever and ever. Amen.

Litany of St. Michael

(For private use.)

Lord, *have mercy on us.*
Christ, *have mercy on us.*

Lord, *have mercy on us.*
Christ, *hear us.*
Christ, *graciously hear us.*

God the Father of heaven, *have mercy on us.*
God the Son, Redeemer of the world, *have mercy on us.*
God the Holy Spirit, *have mercy on us.*
Holy Trinity, one God, *have mercy on us.*

Holy Mary, Queen of Angels, *pray for us.*

St. Michael, filled with the wisdom of God,
   R. *pray for us.*
St. Michael, perfect adorer of the Incarnate Word, **R.**
St. Michael, crowned with honor and glory, **R.**
St. Michael, powerful Prince of the armies of the Lord, **R.**
St. Michael, standard-bearer of the most Holy Trinity, **R.**
St. Michael, guardian of Paradise, **R.**
St. Michael, guide and comforter of God's people, **R.**
St. Michael, splendor and stronghold of the Church on earth, **R.**
St. Michael, honor and joy of the Church in heaven, **R.**
St. Michael, light of angels, **R.**
St. Michael, safeguard of the faithful, **R.**

St. Michael, strength of those struggling against evil forces, **R.**

St. Michael, light and confidence of souls at the hour of death, **R.**

St. Michael, our sure support in time of adversity, **R.**

St. Michael, our help in time of temptation, **R.**

St. Michael, consoler of the souls in purgatory, **R.**

St. Michael, protector of the dying, **R.**

St. Michael, our prince, **R.**

St. Michael, our advocate, **R.**

Lamb of God, you take away the sins of the world, *spare us, O Lord.*

Lamb of God, you take away the sins of the world, *graciously hear us, O Lord.*

Lamb of God, you take away the sins of the world, *have mercy on us.*

V. Pray for us, O glorious St. Michael, prince of the heavenly host.

R. That we may become worthy of the promises of Christ.

Let us pray.

Lord Jesus Christ, through the intercession of St. Michael, grant us the wisdom which teaches us to store treasures in heaven by exchanging the goods of this world for those of eternity, you who live and reign forever and ever. Amen.

Evening Prayer

As this day draws to a close we place ourselves in an attitude of thanksgiving. We take time to express our gratitude to a loving God for his abiding presence. We thank him for the gift of the day and all it brought with it. We thank him for all the things we were able to achieve throughout the day, and we entrust to him the concerns we have for tomorrow.

From the rising to the setting of the sun,
may the name of the Lord be praised.
Glory to the Father, and to the Son, and to the
    Holy Spirit,
as it was in the beginning, is now, and will be
    forever. Amen.

Take a few moments for a brief examination of conscience. Reflect on the ways God acted in your life today; how you responded to his invitations to think, speak, and act in a more Christ-like manner; and in what ways you would like to be a more faithful disciple tomorrow.

In your love and mercy, forgive me, Lord.
For the times I failed to treat others with the dignity they deserve:
Lord, have mercy.
For the times I sinned with my words, by gossip, cutting remarks, untruths, or lack of respect for your holy name:
Christ, have mercy.
For the times I failed to do the good I could have done:
Lord, have mercy.
For the times… *(any other petitions for pardon).*

(Or any other Act of Sorrow.)

Psalm 138

With the angels I will praise you, LORD.
I give you thanks, O LORD, with all my heart,
sing psalms to you in the presence of the angels.
I worship at your holy temple
and praise your name
for your loving kindness and faithfulness.
When I called you answered me,
you gave me courage and strength of soul.

All the rulers of the world, Lord, shall give you thanks,
for they have heard your promises;
they shall sing of the ways of the Lord,
for great is the glory of the Lord.
The Lord is exalted above all, yet cares for the lowly.
Even though I am surrounded by troubles,
you revive me; your right hand saves me.
The Lord will fulfill his promises to me.
O Lord, your loving kindness endures forever.

Glory to the Father….

The Word of God
Exodus 23:20–21

The Lord sends his angels to help us along the way of our lives. If we are attentive, in the silence of our hearts we will hear their inspirations.

I am going to send an angel in front of you, to guard you on the way and to bring you to the place that I have prepared. Be attentive to him and listen to his voice; do not rebel against him, for he will not pardon your transgression; for my name is in him.

Your words, Lord, give joy to my heart.

In prayer we bring before the Lord our own needs and the needs of those we love. We take time to consider the needs of the world and intercede for those who do not or cannot pray. We offer petitions for the improvement of the human condition so that our world will be a better place to live and all people may contribute to building up God's kingdom here on earth.

Intercessions

God our loving Father, as evening falls we come into your presence to thank you for the many ways you have touched our lives today, and we place before you the needs of all humanity.

Response: *Lord, receive our prayer through the intercession of St. Michael.*

That the Pope and all Church leaders may be faithful witnesses to the Gospel, we pray. **R.**

That world leaders may seek peace, promote justice, and strengthen family life, we pray. **R.**

That the Church will be free to proclaim the message of the Gospel in all parts of the world, especially in those areas where Christians now suffer persecution, we pray. **R.**

That children everywhere will experience within their families the love and security they need, we pray. **R.**

That laws will be enacted which protect and value human life at every stage, we pray. **R.**

That the sick and the suffering may experience the touch of the Divine Healer, we pray. **R.**

That all those who struggle with temptation may find victory over sin, we pray. **R.**

For all those who have gone before us in faith, that they may find eternal rest and peace, we pray. **R.**

(Add any other spontaneous intentions and your particular intentions for this novena.)

Conclude your intercessions by praying to our heavenly Father in the words Jesus taught us:

Our Father, who art in heaven…

Closing Prayer

Gracious God, as evening falls and this day draws to a close, we ask you to enfold us in your loving care. We thank you for the many ways you have blessed us today. Grant that we may rest in peace so that tomorrow we may rise strengthened and refreshed to serve you. We ask this through Jesus Christ, your Son. Amen.

Mary, Jesus' Mother and ours, is always ready to intercede for those who ask her help.

Remember, O most gracious Virgin Mary,
that never was it known
that anyone who fled to your protection,
implored your help,
or sought your intercession
was left unaided.
Inspired with this confidence,
I fly to you, O Virgin of virgins, my Mother.
To you I come; before you I stand,
sinful and sorrowful.
O Mother of the Word Incarnate,
despise not my petitions,
but in your mercy hear and answer me. Amen.

May God's blessing remain with us forever. In the name of the Father, and of the Son, and of the Holy Spirit. Amen.

Pauline
BOOKS & MEDIA

The Daughters of St. Paul operate book and media centers at the following addresses. Visit, call or write the one nearest you today, or find us on the World Wide Web, www.pauline.org

CALIFORNIA

3908 Sepulveda Blvd, Culver City, CA 90230 310-397-8676

5945 Balboa Avenue, San Diego, CA 92111 858-565-9181

46 Geary Street, San Francisco, CA 94108 415-781-5180

FLORIDA

145 S.W. 107th Avenue, Miami, FL 33174 305-559-6715

HAWAII

1143 Bishop Street, Honolulu, HI 96813 808-521-2731

Neighbor Islands call: 866-521-2731

ILLINOIS

172 North Michigan Avenue, Chicago, IL 60601 312-346-4228

LOUISIANA

4403 Veterans Memorial Blvd, Metairie, LA 70006 504-887-7631

MASSACHUSETTS

885 Providence Hwy, Dedham, MA 02026 781-326-5385

MISSOURI

9804 Watson Road, St. Louis, MO 63126 314-965-3512

NEW JERSEY

561 U.S. Route 1, Wick Plaza, Edison, NJ 08817 732-572-1200

NEW YORK

150 East 52nd Street, New York, NY 10022 212-754-1110

78 Fort Place, Staten Island, NY 10301 718-447-5071

PENNSYLVANIA

9171-A Roosevelt Blvd, Philadelphia, PA 19114 215-676-9494

SOUTH CAROLINA

243 King Street, Charleston, SC 29401 843-577-0175

TENNESSEE

4811 Poplar Avenue, Memphis, TN 38117 901-761-2987

TEXAS

114 Main Plaza, San Antonio, TX 78205 210-224-8101

VIRGINIA

1025 King Street, Alexandria, VA 22314 703-549-3806

CANADA

3022 Dufferin Street, Toronto, Ontario, Canada M6B 3T5 416-781-9131

1155 Yonge Street, Toronto, Ontario, Canada M4T 1W2 416-934-3440

¡También somos su fuente para libros, videos y música en español!